Making a New Nation

MODERN IMMIGRATION AND EXPANSION

From World War I to September 11

Adam Schaefer

HEINEMANN LIBRARY
CHICAGO, ILLINOIS

Customer Service 888–454–2279

Visit our website at www.heinemannraintree.com

Designed by Philippa Baile and Kim Miracle
Maps by Jeff Edwards
Printed and bound in the United States, North Mankato, Minnesota.

12 11 10
10 9 8 7 6 5 4 3

Library of Congress Cataloging-in-Publication Data
Schaefer, A. R. (Adam Richard), 1976-
  Modern immigration and expansion / Adam Schaefer.
     p. cm. -- (Making a new nation)
  Includes bibliographical references and index.
  ISBN 1-4034-7831-7 (library binding-hardcover) -- ISBN 978-1-4034-7838-2 (pbk.)
  1. United States--Emigration and immigration--History--Juvenile literature.
I. Title. II. Series.
  JV6450.S34 2006
  304.8'73--dc22

                              2006003252

Acknowledgments
The author and publisher are grateful to the following for permission to reproduce copyright material: AKG-Images p. **19** (Ullstein Bild), **9**, **10**, **24**; Corbis pp. **16** (Charles E. Rotkin), **18**, **21** (Dorothea Lange), **35** (Ramin Talaie), **37** (George Hall), **17**, **20**; Corbis/Bettmann pp. **4**, **12**, **14**, **28**, **31**; Getty Images pp. **34** (Peter C. Brandt), **42** (Mario Tama); Getty Images/Photodisc p. **5**; Getty Images/Time Life Pictures pp. **26** (Ed Clark), **27** (Leonard McCombe); Mary Evans Picture Library p. **11**; Still Pictures pp. **32** (Jeff Greenberg), **39** (Jim Wark); Topfoto p. **15**; Topfoto/ImageWorks p. **40**; Topham Picturepoint pp. **8**, **23**.

Cover photograph reproduced with the permission of Shannon Stapleton/Reuters/Corbis.

The publishers would like to thank Jarod Roll of Northwestern University for his help in the preparation of this book.

082010
005845RP

CONTENTS

Some words are shown in bold, **like this**. You can find out what they mean by looking in the glossary.

LAND OF IMMIGRANTS

For many years, the lands of North America were open to anyone who wanted to come in search of a better life. Millions of **immigrants** came. By about 1900, some United States **citizens** started to feel that immigration was not such a good idea. For the first time, the nation's doors began to be closed to immigrants.

The story of immigration in the United States had begun thousands of years earlier. The first inhabitants of North America, the Native Americans, crossed a **land bridge** from Asia. They soon spread throughout the continent. European **settlers** arrived in the 1500s in another wave of immigration. The British, Dutch, French, and Spanish governments soon started **colonies** in North America.

People from other countries also came to the American colonies during this time. Most were hoping to buy land and make a better life for their families. But not everyone chose to come. Hundreds of thousands of Africans were brought to the colonies. They were forced to come and work in **slavery**.

St. Augustine, Florida, was founded by the Spanish in 1565. It was the first European settlement in the land that is now the United States.

IMMIGRATION IN A NEW COUNTRY

In 1788, twelve years after the United States became independent, its people agreed on a **constitution**. One of the powers it gave the government was the power to control immigration. The first **census** of the new nation took place in 1790. It showed that about 64 percent of the country was of British origin. About 20 percent was of African origin—mostly slaves—and 7 percent was of German origin.

For many immigrants to the U.S., the Statue of Liberty was their first sight of their new country.

EUROPEAN BOOM

The first large immigration boom into the United States started in the 1840s. Most of these immigrants were from Western and Northern Europe. This increase in immigration was due, in part, to problems in Europe. Some people did not have enough food to eat. Others wanted to leave for a country with more freedoms.

In 1882 **Congress** passed the Chinese Exclusion Act, which restricted Chinese immigration. **Federal** law was also changed to keep out criminals, people with mental disabilities, and people the government thought would become a burden on society.

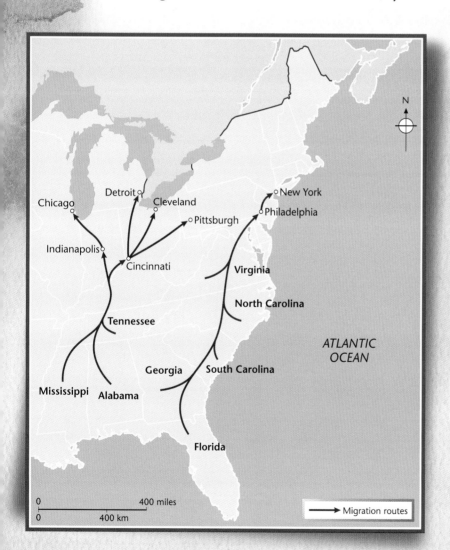

The Great Migration occurred in the years before 1920.

Immigration and migration

While immigrants were settling in different parts of the U.S., citizens were moving around, or migrating, within the country as well. A large shift occurred during World War I (1914–1918). Factories that produced war equipment were mostly located in northern cities. They needed workers and paid good wages. Many African Americans moved north with their families. This became known as the Great Migration.

IMMIGRATION IN THE 1900S

The immigration rate did not slow down after the changes in the law. Many of the immigrants in the early 1900s were from Southern and Eastern Europe. The United States also admitted a large number of people from Mexico.

Many immigrants wanted to be around other people from their home countries. In large cities, there were often neighborhoods with **ethnic** names, such as Little Italy and Chinatown. These clusters existed on a larger scale as well. Many people from Scandinavian countries settled in the upper Midwest, while the Great Lakes region was populated with Germans and Poles.

The United States was founded by immigrants, but some of the **descendants** of those immigrants changed the laws to keep others out. During the same time period, the country experienced many other changes. People moved from south to north, and from city to suburb. Immigration changed in the 1900s, and **migration** at that time shaped the nation as we know it today.

These thirteen western states entered the United States from 1864 to 1912.

States admitted to the Union 1787–1863

States added 1864–1912

TURNING AGAINST IMMIGRATION

Immigration had grown rapidly during the second half of the 1800s. Most immigrants worked hard to become good citizens in their new country. However, not everyone wanted them in the U.S. As more and more immigrants entered the United States, anti-immigrant feelings rose.

Some U.S. citizens grew angry at people moving into their country. They did not like how immigrants spoke their native languages, had their own schools, and read their own newspapers. These people were part of the nativism movement. **Nativists** wanted immigration to slow down or stop. They wanted to make it harder to become a U.S. citizen.

U.S. troops fought in Europe during World War I.

Enemies and languages

"If a man cannot speak English, and can only speak German, that man must be an enemy of the United States because he does not understand this wonderful **democracy** of ours. But if a man can speak English and prefers to speak German, then since it is war time, that man must be doubly an enemy of the United States."
– U.S. Army Sgt. Arthur Guy Empey in *McClure's* (magazine), July 1917

ANTI-GERMAN FEELING

World War I was a difficult time for many German immigrants. German Americans had ties to their native country. There were German newspapers, schools, and social clubs. When the United States and Germany fought each other in World War I, many Americans questioned the loyalties of German immigrants who were still so strongly connected to German culture.

This suspicion of German Americans led to action in many places. Local governments changed German-sounding town, street, and park names. German music was not played at concerts. German immigrants stopped buying newspapers in their native language. German schools were closed and German books were burned. In some places, homes and businesses of German immigrants were attacked and some people were even hurt physically.

The United States fought against Germany in World War I.

OurFlags

BEAT GERMANY
Support EVERY FLAG
that opposes Prussianism
Eat less of the food Fighters need
DENY yourself something
WASTE NOTHING

UNITED STATES FOOD ADMINISTRATION

EXCLUDING ASIANS

The Germans were not the first immigrants to face hatred. In the late 1800s, many Asians, mainly Chinese, had settled in the United States. Like the Germans, many Asians kept traditions from their home countries. They also had close-knit communities. In addition, it was easy for people to tell Asians apart from other people, whereas Germans did not look very different from other Europeans. Many nativists did not want Asians in the country. In 1882 the U.S. government passed the Chinese Exclusion Act. This law **prohibited** the admission of Chinese immigrants into the country.

Asians were a target of the anti-immigration movement of the late 1800s.

Violence in the West

Anti-immigrant feeling sometimes turned into violence. During the late 1800s, Chinese immigrants were the target of several race riots in the western United States. The worst was in Rock Springs, in the Wyoming **Territory**. On September 2, 1885, 150 armed men attacked Chinese mine workers in Rock Springs. They killed 28, hurt 15 more, and drove hundreds away from the area.

THE LITERACY TEST

At the end of the 1800s, large numbers of Southern and Eastern Europeans moved to the United States. Their languages and customs were very different from the people who had immigrated from Northern and Western Europe. Many Americans wrongly thought that these new immigrants were lazy, unintelligent, diseased, and criminal. Nativists pushed for a **literacy** test to be given to incoming immigrants. In 1917 Congress passed a law that required just that. Incoming immigrants had to prove that they could read and write before being admitted to the United States.

THEY COME ARM IN ARM.
American seaports must close their gates to all three.

Some Americans were worried about immigrants bringing diseases to the U.S., as this cartoon shows.

BETWEEN THE WARS

Nativists pushed for changes to immigration rules throughout the 1920s. European immigration had slowed during World War I, but it increased again in the early 1920s. However, it was still not as high as it had been. This was due to the literacy test and other laws. There were also changes to migration within the United States.

SETTING LIMITS

In 1921 a new federal law established immigration **quotas** for the first time. This law limited the number of people who could be admitted from a certain country each year. The limit was based on the percentage of people from that country who were already in the United States. The effect of the quota law was to make sure that the ethnic makeup of the country would not change a lot. The law also capped European immigration at 350,000 persons each year.

After legal changes in the 1920s, immigration was mostly available to white Europeans, such as this family from Ireland.

IMMIGRATION DROPS

In 1924 nativists were successful in making the quota even tighter. That year, Congress passed laws that made it difficult for people to immigrate to the United States. First, it lowered the quota numbers for all countries of the world. Second, it prohibited Japanese and other northern Asian immigration. It also set a limit of 165,000 immigrants a year from European countries. In 1927 this was reduced to 150,000. In 1929 the quota laws passed in 1924 were made permanent.

Major laws between 1917 and 1929

1917   Immigration Act of 1917
Excluded persons from India and other South Asian countries from admission. Also introduced a literacy test.

1921   1921 Quota Act
Congress introduces a quota system. It limits the number of people that can be admitted from any one country.

1924   1924 National Origins Quota Act
Excluded Japanese from admission. Tightened up the quotas, allowing fewer people to be admitted.

1929   Congress makes the quotas from 1924 permanent.

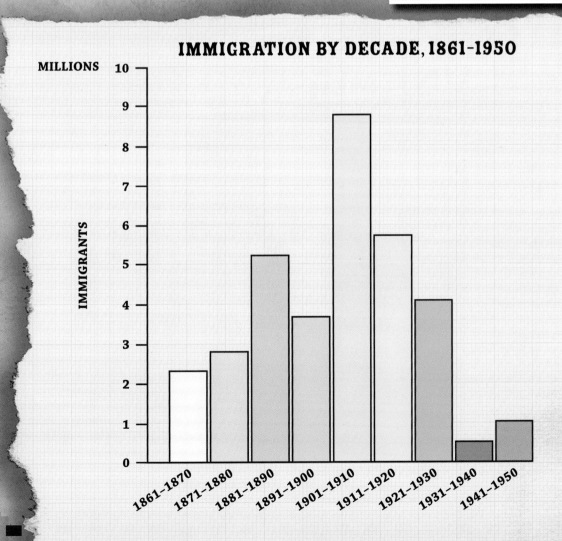

IMMIGRATION BY DECADE, 1861–1950

MILLIONS

IMMIGRANTS

1861–1870 · 1871–1880 · 1881–1890 · 1891–1900 · 1901–1910 · 1911–1920 · 1921–1930 · 1931–1940 · 1941–1950

THE GREAT DEPRESSION

Something else happened in 1929 that changed how many people were immigrating to the United States. In October, the U.S. **stock market** collapsed, causing the Great Depression. Many people lost their savings, houses, and jobs. The unemployment rate was the highest in U.S. history. Suddenly, the United States was no longer the land of opportunity. There were no jobs for citizens or immigrants.

Over the next decade, immigration into the U.S. shrank to less than 100,000 people per year. This happened for two main reasons. The Great Depression made the country less attractive to immigrants, and the immigration laws made it hard for people who did want to come to the country.

Many people were without work and sometimes food during the Great Depression.

MIGRATING NORTH

People did, however, increasingly move around within the United States. After the Civil War and the **emancipation** of slaves, most African Americans continued to live in the southern United States. When an insect destroyed the southern cotton crop around 1900, many African Americans decided to move north.

In fact, the promise of good jobs and a better life drove many more African Americans to move out of the South. Between 1910 and 1930, the African-American population of the North grew by as much as 20 percent. Large African-American communities grew in northern cities such as Philadelphia, Chicago, Cleveland, and Detroit.

The Harlem Renaissance was centered around the arts and culture of African Americans.

Harlem Renaissance
During the 1920s, Harlem was the center of an African-American arts, **commerce**, and literature movement. It became known as the Harlem Renaissance. African Americans from all over the United States, but particularly the South, moved to Harlem, in New York City. They started businesses, wrote books, painted, played music, and published magazines. Harlem was also a place where the **civil rights** movement grew in the U.S.

THE RISE OF COMPANY TOWNS

In the 1900s, company towns could be found throughout the United States. A company town is a town entirely owned and operated by a single company. Large businesses such as steel and mining companies needed thousands of workers. They were often in rural, undeveloped locations. Their solution was to build a completely new town.

The companies built everything needed for a town: homes, schools, stores, and parks. Only employees and their families lived in company towns. They bought or rented homes from the business. The families purchased food and clothes from company-owned stores. The business hired teachers for the schools.

Other cities were thought of as company towns, but they were not officially company towns. Instead, they were regular towns that grew around one central business. In these towns, the stores and homes were owned by individuals rather than by the company. However, the people of these towns still depended on one main company for almost all of the jobs.

Company towns were owned and operated by large businesses.

The company store

"You walked in the company store and it was fairly big...The post-office was in the store at the time. As you came in the main door and made a sharp left turn the butcher shop was there separated from the rest of the store. During the period of time when the days were bad for coal mines, just about everybody that worked in the mines owed their money to the company store." A memory of McIntyre, Pennsylvania.

Company stores sold everything that the company's employees needed.

THE DUST BOWL

U.S. cities and towns are only part of the story of migration during this period. Many farmers had moved to the Midwest and Great Plains when the U.S. expanded in the 1800s. They had cleared trees and grasses from the land in these areas. The soil was full of **nutrients** and crops grew well. But after many years, planting and harvesting again and again drained the soil of nutrients. Plants did not grow as well. A low rainfall led to drought. Nothing grew in the dry earth. Large patches of land were bare and open to the wind. The wind dried out the earth even more, then picked it up into the air.

Dust storms ravaged the Great Plains. The Plains became known as the Dust Bowl. It was impossible to grow anything. Sometimes the dust storms were so bad that people could barely see anything outdoors. With no soil and no water, a farmer could no longer make a living. During the 1930s, thousands of farmers and their families packed up all of their belongings and moved. Many went to California, where they heard there were lush, green valleys for growing food.

The Dust Bowl forced people to leave their homes.

REASONS FOR MIGRATION

Large-scale migration can occur for a variety of reasons. Availability of good jobs in an area is an example of a reason people might move to a place. Not having freedom of religion is an example of why a person might move away from a place. The rise of the automobile was another large factor in U.S. migration.

The Okies

Oklahoma was hit hard by drought and the Depression. Hundreds of thousands of people from Oklahoma left the state and traveled west. Many went to California and Oregon. Some people looked down on them because they were poor. They became known as Okies. The tale of the Okies was made famous in John Steinbeck's book *The Grapes of Wrath*.

When cars and trucks became affordable, many Americans had the means to migrate wherever they wanted.

WORLD WAR II

As the United States came out of the Great Depression in the late 1930s, the possibility of war increased. Germany, Italy, and Japan were taking positions against U.S. **allies**. The U.S. entered World War II (1939–1945) in 1941. Many Americans again questioned the loyalties of German and Italian Americans. As was the case during World War I, German words were removed from the U.S. vocabulary.

The U.S. government printed materials encouraging Americans to work hard for the war effort.

CONCERN ABOUT JAPANESE

Japanese Americans, however, had it much worse than German and Italian Americans. Although there had been limits on Japanese immigration for decades, there were still large Japanese communities on the west coast. After Japan bombed Pearl Harbor in Hawaii in 1941, killing many Americans, some people worried that Japanese Americans would be loyal to Japan. Much of this was based on nothing more than **racism**.

INTERNMENT CAMPS

Over the next several months, between 112,000 and 120,000 Japanese Americans were ordered to leave their homes. These people were sent to **internment camps** in the West. Most of those interned were citizens who had been born in the United States. Some of them challenged the orders all the way to the **Supreme Court**. That court said that the government could keep them in internment camps because of the war.

Apologies and payments

After the war was over, many Japanese families tried to make the government pay for the loss of their land and belongings. The U.S. government paid many of these families. In the 1980s, the government officially apologized to the people who were interned. It paid $20,000 to each surviving detainee.

More than 100,000 Japanese Americans were taken to internment camps during World War II.

NOWHERE TO GO

World War II made many families in Europe homeless. Some people from other nations were trying to enter the United States. For example, Jewish people in areas controlled by the Germans were being killed. Many of them tried to leave Europe and make their way to the United States. These people were **refugees**. Refugees try to leave a place because they are being threatened. Many of them try to move to new countries.

The federal law on immigration had not changed since 1929. This meant that it was very difficult for Eastern Europeans to immigrate legally to the United States. There were times when people escaped the Nazis and made it on a ship to the U.S. But when they arrived, the U.S. government would not admit them. They were shipped back to Europe, where many of them were later killed.

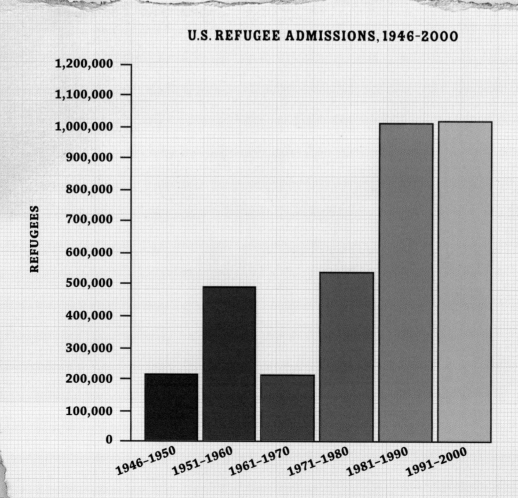

U.S. REFUGEE ADMISSIONS, 1946-2000

HELPING THE REFUGEES

Some people thought that the United States should change the law to help people who were being forced out of their homes in Europe. A bill was introduced in Congress, but it did not pass. Finally, President Franklin D. Roosevelt and his administration made a change in policy. Under the new rules, many refugees who were fleeing the war were allowed to immigrate to the United States. This policy continued for several years after the war was over.

Refugees were trying to escape death and concentration camps in Europe.

A refugee's tale

"So I managed to sneak across the border into West Germany...and worked as an interrogator/translator for American intelligence which is where I met my wife.... We didn't want to stay and always be worried about the threat of war. We thought maybe we'd go to Australia or Canada...But when President [Harry S.] Truman enacted the Refugee Act into law we thought it would be easier to go to the United States." William Denovak emigrated from Czechoslovakia in 1953. From *Ellis Island Interviews: In Their Own Words*. Peter Morton Coan, ed. New York: Facts On File, Inc., 1997.

LIFE AFTER THE WAR

During World War II, U.S. factories operated at full production to supply troops with machines and supplies. By the time the war ended, the war had pushed the U.S. **economy** into a strong position.

The 1950s were a time of **prosperity** in the United States. Many returning soldiers found good jobs in factories. Others studied under the G.I. Bill (see page 25) and found better jobs. Their new, young families had the money to afford automobiles. Traditional homes in large cities were expensive. Many of these young families also did not want to live in crowded cities with high crime. So, they moved to the suburbs.

The suburbs offered people more room and a place to park their car.

LIFE IN THE SUBURBS

A suburb is a small community positioned near a bigger city. People who live in suburbs often shop, work, and have fun in the larger city. Before the war, suburbs existed in only a few places throughout the United States. Living several miles outside of a city would have been difficult before cars became popular. But in the 1950s, many young families had automobiles. They found property to be cheaper outside of the large cities. They could afford more land. There was less crime. The schools, stores, and houses were newer.

To many people, leaving city centers for the suburbs was the new American dream. They hoped for the possibility of a big house and a large yard. Other people saw the rise of the suburbs as a serious social problem known as "white flight." The people who had the means to leave cities did so. Urban living in most parts of the country became associated with being poor and being part of a minority.

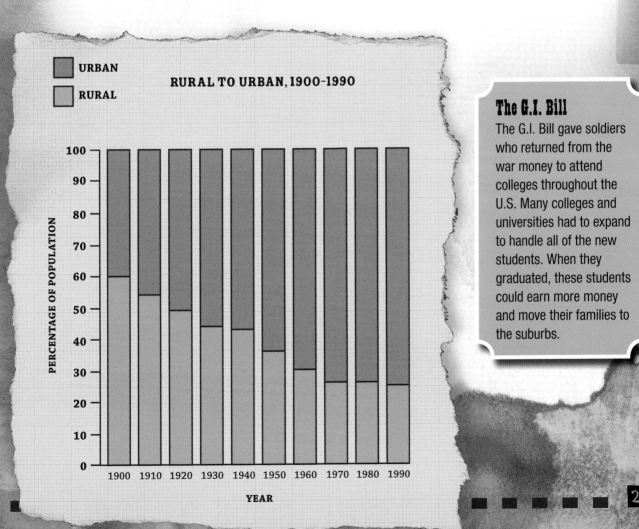

URBAN
RURAL

RURAL TO URBAN, 1900–1990

PERCENTAGE OF POPULATION

YEAR

The G.I. Bill
The G.I. Bill gave soldiers who returned from the war money to attend colleges throughout the U.S. Many colleges and universities had to expand to handle all of the new students. When they graduated, these students could earn more money and move their families to the suburbs.

EXPANSION OF THE UNION

During the 1950s, the **borders** of the United States were pushed
to new limits. To the north, Alaska had been purchased by
the U.S. government from Russia back in 1867. At first, many
people considered the purchase a mistake. They thought that the
government had paid a large amount of money for a place too cold for
people or animals to live. Later, large amounts of gold, oil, and other
natural resources were discovered in Alaska. Congress approved
making Alaska a state in 1958.

*President Dwight D. Eisenhower signed
the bill that made Alaska a state in 1959.*

HAWAII

The kingdom of Hawaii had been an independent country until the late 1800s. Some U.S. businesses realized that Hawaii had tropical soil and weather perfect for growing crops. With the help of the U.S. military, they overthrew the Hawaiian queen, Liliuokalani. The U.S. government claimed Hawaii as a territory in 1898. For many years, it was home to important U.S. military bases. After World War II, many Americans realized how important Hawaii was to the United States. People on the mainland and in Hawaii pushed for statehood.

Hawaii and Alaska were the first and only states that are not **contiguous** with other U.S. territory. Neither one of them touch other U.S. states. Both Alaska and Hawaii are closer to other countries than they are to the U.S. mainland. In addition, both states have large non-white populations. In Alaska, native Alaskan tribes make up a significant percentage of the population. Asians and native Hawaiians made up the majority of Hawaii's people. These were the first states admitted with a majority of non-white free people.

Hawaii became the 50th state in the United States in 1959.

Space exploration

The 1950s and 1960s were also an important time in the U.S. space program. At that time, space was seen as the next **frontier**. People spoke of large developments on the moon and on the other planets of our solar system. The United States sent people into orbit and eventually to visit the moon.

IMMIGRATION REFORM

After World War II, many people felt that racism was wrong. They thought it was one of the causes of war. These people wanted to make sure that what happened in Europe could not happen in the United States. In the 1950s and 1960s, these concerns were the center of public debate. The civil rights movement in the U.S. helped protect the rights of minorities living in the United States.

END OF THE QUOTAS

Immigration policy was also examined. The Chinese Exclusion Act was repealed (ended) in 1943, but the quota system from 1929 was still in effect. This meant that even though Asians were not all **excluded**, very few were allowed to enter legally. This was also true of other racial minorities. Many people felt that this was wrong.

President Lyndon B. Johnson worked with Congress to pass a bill in 1965 that changed the law. That legislation removed many of the old rules.

President Lyndon B. Johnson opened U.S. doors to more immigrants when he signed the Immigration Reform Act of 1965.

IMMIGRATION GOES BACK UP

As soon as the law went into effect, there was an increase in the number of people admitted to the country. In 1961, before the law was passed, only 271,344 people were admitted into the United States. Ten years later, after the new law, that number was more than 370,000. The number of people allowed to enter the country has continued to grow each decade since.

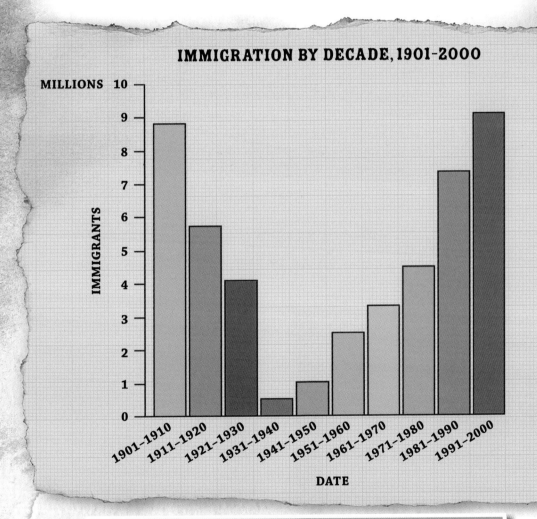

IMMIGRATION BY DECADE, 1901-2000

MILLIONS

IMMIGRANTS

DATE

Action hero immigrant

Arnold Schwarzenegger is one of the success stories of U.S. immigration. Schwarzenegger was born in 1947 in Austria and moved to the United States in 1968. He became a bodybuilder and won several world titles. This made him famous; later, he became a well-known movie actor. He became a U.S. citizen in 1983. In 2003 he was elected governor of California. To many people, he represents the possibilities that exist for immigrants in the United States.

THE COLD WAR

After World War II, the world was loosely divided into two groups. On one side were **capitalist** nations and their allies, led by the United States. On the other side were **communist** nations and their allies, led by the **Soviet Union**. The United States and the Soviet Union were considered the world's two great countries. They never declared war and fought head-to-head, but the two countries argued and came close to war several times. This was known as the Cold War.

The Cold War greatly affected how the U.S. dealt with immigration. Many communist countries had closed borders. This meant that the people living in those nations were not free to leave. Most people who lived in communist countries did not have very good living conditions. They did not make much money. They were not allowed to practice religion. People tried to escape to nations that allowed more freedom. The United States represented that freedom to many people.

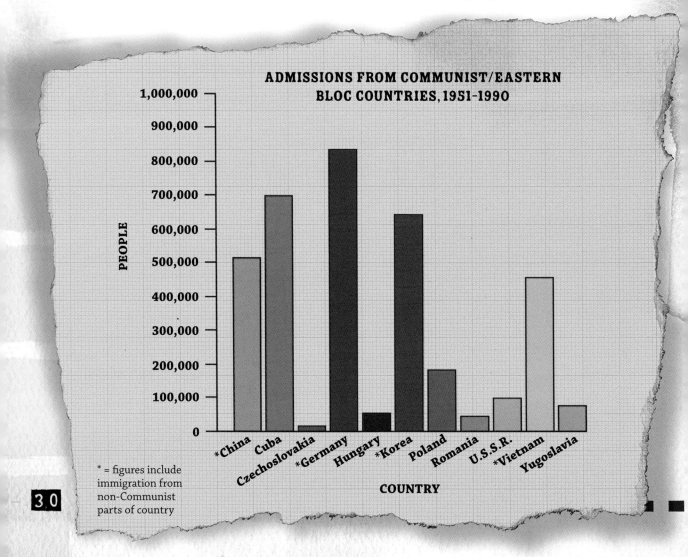

ADMISSIONS FROM COMMUNIST/EASTERN BLOC COUNTRIES, 1951–1990

* = figures include immigration from non-Communist parts of country

WELCOMING REFUGEES

In many cases, the United States welcomed these religious and **political** immigrants. The U.S. government said that they showed why capitalist countries were better than communist societies. In 1957 Congress passed the Refugee Escape Act. This law allowed people who left a communist country or the Middle East to enter the United States.

In the 1950s, thousands of Korean refugees left that nation. They left to escape the war between communist North Korea and capitalist South Korea. Something similar happened in the 1960s and 1970s in Southeast Asia. Refugees to the U.S. came mostly from Vietnam, Laos, and Cambodia.

Cuba

Cuba is a large island in the Caribbean Sea that played an important role in the Cold War and in U.S. immigration. Cuba is just 90 miles (145 kilometers) from Florida and is a communist country. During the Cold War, it was an ally of the Soviet Union. This made it an enemy of the U.S. Still, the United States accepted many Cuban immigrants for political reasons.

Many Cubans have sailed to Florida to make it into the United States.

IMMIGRATION FROM THE NEW WORLD

The makeup of U.S. immigrants changed after the government got rid of the quota law in 1965. In the immigration boom between 1850 and 1920, most immigrants were from Europe. But in the 1960s, several hundred thousand more immigrants arrived from the Americas than from Europe. In the late 1960s and early 1970s, the number of immigrants coming from Asia also passed the number coming from Europe. Large numbers of Mexicans, Filipinos, and Vietnamese arrived instead of Germans, Italians, and British.

In the 1990s, almost one million more Mexicans moved to the United States than Europeans. Asian immigration also rose. Large numbers of immigrants from India and the Philippines moved to the United States.

There are large Cuban-American communities in Miami and New York City.

CHANGES IN IMMIGRATION

The way immigrants arrived also changed. European immigrants used to arrive on large steamer ships that crossed the Atlantic Ocean and sailed into U.S. harbors. The new wave of immigration often came over land or in airplanes.

These new immigrants have settled all over the United States. Many Mexicans and Central Americans moved to the Southwest, part of which used to belong to Mexico. Others settled in rural areas in the Midwest and South. People from the Caribbean often settled in large cities, creating ethnic neighborhoods. The Puerto Rican, Jamaican, and Cuban areas of cities such as Miami, Florida, and New York City are similar to the German and Italian neighborhoods that existed at the turn of the century.

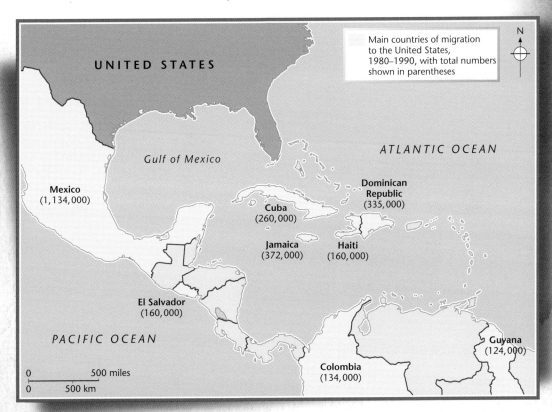

Many recent immigrants to the United States have come from Central America and the Caribbean.

Puerto Rico

Puerto Rico has a unique place in U.S. immigration history. This Caribbean island is a Spanish-speaking U.S. possession. About two million people moved from Puerto Rico to the U.S. in the 1900s. Many of them settled in New York City and Miami. Today, people from other Caribbean nations are moving to Puerto Rico because of its close connection with the United States.

SEPTEMBER 11 AND IMMIGRATION

On September 11, 2001, nineteen members of the **terrorist** group Al-Qaeda took over four airplanes in the U.S. They flew two of them into the World Trade Center in New York City. One was flown into the Pentagon in Washington, D.C. The fourth crashed into a field in Pennsylvania. About 3,000 people were killed. Because of this, the United States government declared a "global war on terror."

Like other conflicts in history, this one affected U.S. immigration policy. None of the September 11 terrorists were U.S. citizens. All had been admitted into the country legally, but some of them had stayed too long, making them illegal. Still, many people looked at the attacks as a failure of immigration laws. Politicians and citizens demanded that something be done.

The attack on the World Trade Center on September 11, 2001 sparked a debate about immigration in the U.S.

TOUGHER ENFORCEMENT

Soon after the attacks, changes were made to immigration rules. The government body in charge of immigration became part of the newly formed Department of Homeland Security (DHS). DHS is responsible for the safety of the United States. The agency started enforcing laws more strictly. Congress also changed some laws. These changes make it easier for DHS to exclude or **deport** anyone suspected of having ties to terrorism.

Many people wanted to restrict immigration from the Middle East, since that is where the September 11 hijackers came from. Other people said that a new law like this would be racist and wrong. So far, no law like this has been passed.

The United States began tougher enforcement of immigration laws after 2001.

History repeated

Soon after September 11, the U.S. government detained (held for questioning) hundreds of immigrants and visitors from other countries. The government said that these people might know something about terrorism in the United States. Some people were soon released. Some were taken back to their country of origin. Others have been held by the government for years without trials. This led some people to compare the treatment of these people to the Japanese during World War II.

CURRENT TRENDS IN IMMIGRATION

Immigration to the United States today is both similar and very different from what it was like 100 years ago. At that time, almost all immigrants were Europeans. They arrived in U.S. ports on large ships. Asian immigrants were excluded from the country. Today, some immigrants still arrive on ships, and some are still European. But most immigrants are from the Americas and Asia. Many arrive over land or in airplanes. People from almost every country can move to the United States to live and work.

The U.S. Citizenship and Immigration Services (USCIS) is the federal government agency in charge of immigration. The USCIS carries out the current immigration laws. The current law allows people who fit many different categories to enter the U.S. Some of the people are family members of U.S. citizens and residents. Some are people who have skills that are needed in the U.S. Others are refugees from political or religious problems in other parts of the world.

Today, immigrants come from around the world to live and work in the United States. In 2003 the country sending the most immigrants to the U.S. was Mexico. It was followed by India, the Philippines, and China.

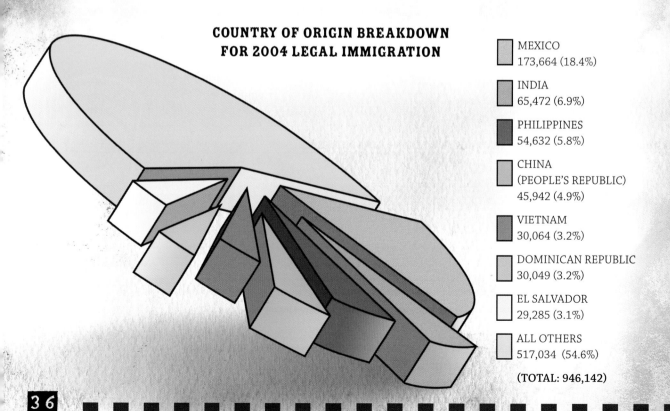

COUNTRY OF ORIGIN BREAKDOWN FOR 2004 LEGAL IMMIGRATION

MEXICO
173,664 (18.4%)

INDIA
65,472 (6.9%)

PHILIPPINES
54,632 (5.8%)

CHINA
(PEOPLE'S REPUBLIC)
45,942 (4.9%)

VIETNAM
30,064 (3.2%)

DOMINICAN REPUBLIC
30,049 (3.2%)

EL SALVADOR
29,285 (3.1%)

ALL OTHERS
517,034 (54.6%)

(TOTAL: 946,142)

Today, many immigrants arrive in the U.S. on airplanes.

Long wait

Many people who would like to immigrate to the United States legally have to wait a while to do so. If they apply for admission in a category that has filled its quota for a year, they will not be allowed in that year. The U.S. government makes a waiting list in the order that people file for admission. In some categories, the list is very long. This means that some people wait for several years before gaining admission into the country.

CURRENT TRENDS IN MIGRATION

During the last twenty years, there has been a large population shift inside the United States. Like other times in the nation's history, people have left their homes to look for a better life in other parts of the country.

One of the largest recent migrations in the United States has been from the Midwest to the Southeast. Large midwestern cities once depended on factories and heavy industry for jobs. For example, Detroit, Michigan, used to be the center of the U.S. car industry. In the late 1970s and 1980s, some of these factories went out of business. Other factories moved to other places. People who lived in these areas lost their jobs. Many of them moved to other parts of the country to find work.

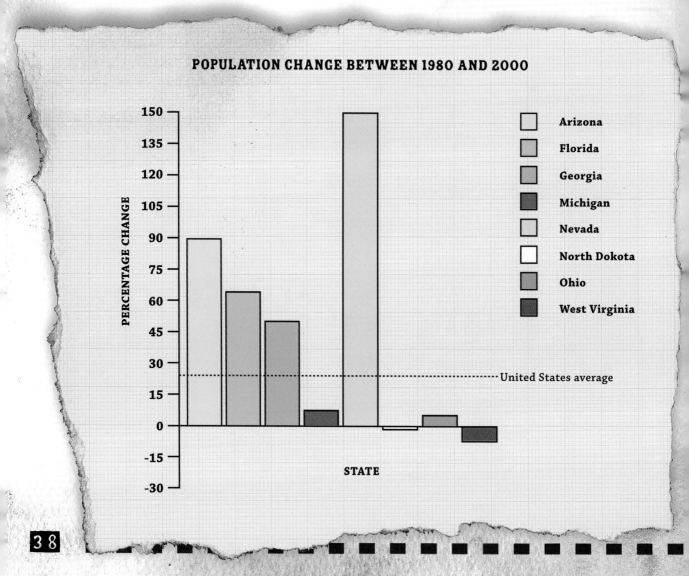

POPULATION CHANGE BETWEEN 1980 AND 2000

PERCENTAGE CHANGE

STATE

United States average

- Arizona
- Florida
- Georgia
- Michigan
- Nevada
- North Dokota
- Ohio
- West Virginia

A SHIFT IN ECONOMY

At the same time, the United States has shifted from an industrial economy to a service economy. An industrial company makes things. These companies are usually located near transportation systems and natural resources. Service companies sell services or things that people do for each other or for businesses. Service companies can be more flexible with their locations. Many choose to be in areas with good weather.

As manufacturing companies closed in the Midwest, service companies opened in the Southeast and Southwest. People moved to follow the jobs. Between 1980 and 2000, the state of Florida grew by 64 percent and the population of Nevada grew almost 150 percent.

A town in a city

Planned communities, also called new towns, greenbelt towns, or garden cities, are not a new idea. Some ancient Greeks may have been the first people to plan their entire village before it was built. But today, planned communities are growing up all over the United States. In a planned community, there is a plan for everything before construction begins. Everyone knows where schools, stores, and houses will be and how they will look before they are built.

Many Americans now live in suburbs.

DEBATES ABOUT IMMIGRATION

The United States adds more than half a million legal immigrants to its population each year. Some Americans think that is too many. They say that the United States is not doing a good job with the people that already live in the country. These people are worried about the number of jobs available. They think that adding more people puts a strain on services like education, transportation, and health care.

Some Americans are for open immigration. They see the United States as a land of immigration. They say that the U.S. is a mixture of people and cultures from all over the world.

Others like things the way they are. They want some immigration into the U.S, but they also want it limited to a certain number each year. Under this system, the United States is still open to the world, but the yearly limits help the country adjust to its new residents.

The issue of immigration from Mexico leads to heated debate in the U.S.

THE ILLEGAL QUESTION

There may be as many as ten million people living in the United States illegally. Many of them snuck across the border. Other people came legally but did not leave when they should have. Many Americans are against illegal immigration.

Terrorism is also an important issue in immigration. Most of the September 11, 2001, hijackers were in the United States illegally. Some Americans are worried that illegal immigrants could attack inside the country again.

ESTIMATED UNAUTHORIZED IMMIGRATION SINCE 1985

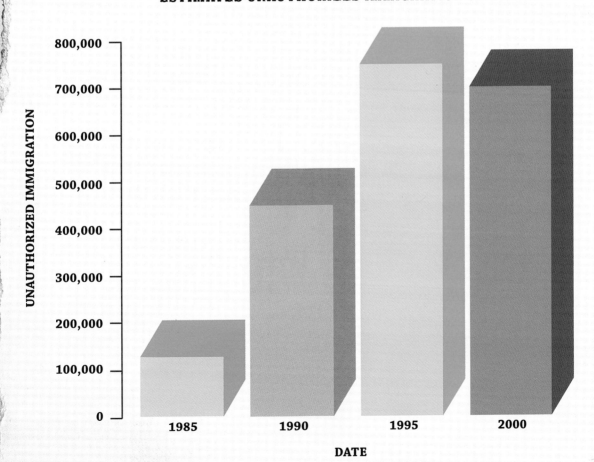

ONE NATION, TWO LANGUAGES

Many immigrants today are Spanish-speaking. Street signs are now required to be in English and Spanish in some cities. While some Americans believe that all immigrants should learn to speak English, others point out that the same things were said about Germans and other immigrant groups many years ago.

Immigration will continue to be an important issue in the United States. If the current trends continue, more than half of the people in the United States may speak Spanish by 2050. People living in Puerto Rico speak Spanish. Some Puerto Ricans want the island to become independent of the United States. Others would like it to become the 51st state, while still others want things to stay the way they are.

In many places, signs are in two languages so that Spanish-speaking immigrants can read them.

THE UNITED STATES TODAY

Today, the United States stands at 50 states. It also has a number of possessions around the world, such as Puerto Rico and the U.S. Virgin Islands. Some are tiny and uninhabited, such as Kingman Reef in the Pacific Ocean. It is a tiny strip of land with no people and no buildings.

If current trends continue, the United States will continue to grow. Immigrants will move to the country. People in the country will migrate from one area to another. Immigration will continue to be a subject of debate, just as it has been for centuries in the United States.

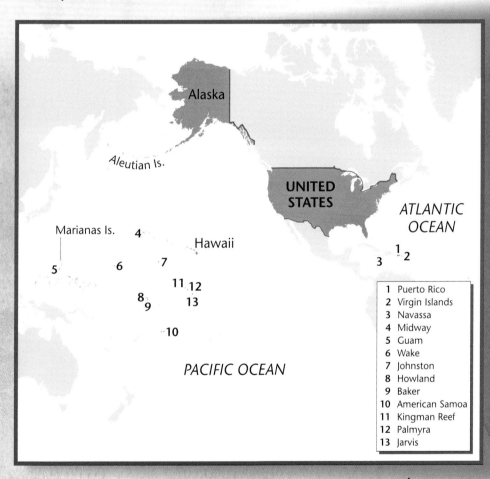

The U.S. occupies a number of territories around the world.

1 Puerto Rico
2 Virgin Islands
3 Navassa
4 Midway
5 Guam
6 Wake
7 Johnston
8 Howland
9 Baker
10 American Samoa
11 Kingman Reef
12 Palmyra
13 Jarvis

Occupied territories

At many times during the history of the United States, the government has controlled areas in other parts of the world. Sometimes they become territories and later states. This happened in Hawaii. Other times, such as with the Philippines, they become independent.

IMMIGRATION BY REGION

Over the years, the number of immigrants has changed. So have the places they came from. In 1900 most immigrants came from Europe. Now, they are outnumbered by arrivals from Asia and the Americas.

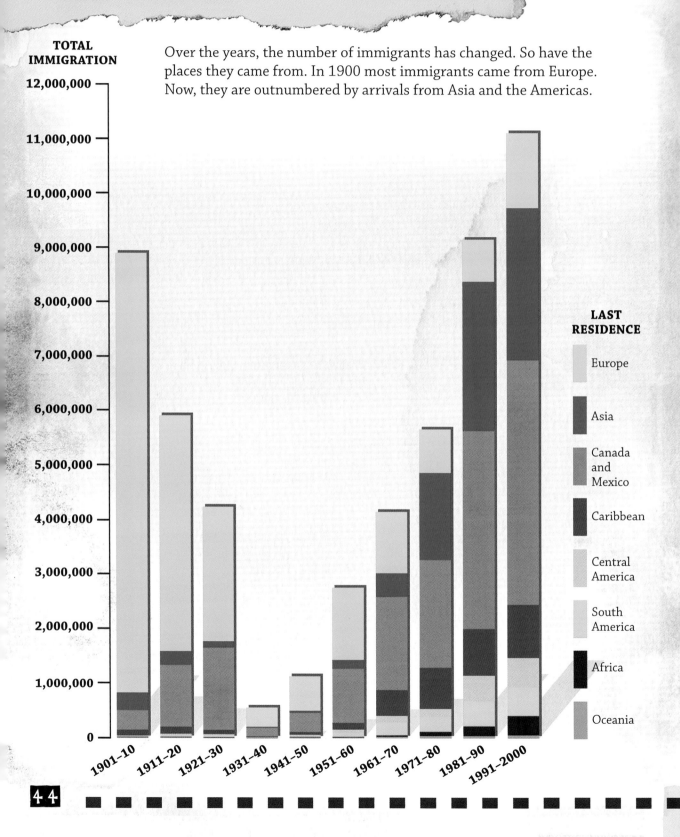

TOTAL IMMIGRATION

12,000,000
11,000,000
10,000,000
9,000,000
8,000,000
7,000,000
6,000,000
5,000,000
4,000,000
3,000,000
2,000,000
1,000,000
0

1901–10　1911–20　1921–30　1931–40　1941–50　1951–60　1961–70　1971–80　1981–90　1991–2000

LAST RESIDENCE

- Europe
- Asia
- Canada and Mexico
- Caribbean
- Central America
- South America
- Africa
- Oceania

TIMELINE

1882 Congress passes Chinese Exclusion Act, keeping Chinese immigrants from entering the United States.

1917 The United States enters World War I; Congress passes the literacy test requirement for incoming immigrants.

1921 A new federal law begins the quota system of admitting immigrants.

1924 The National Origins Act makes tighter quotas, and as a result these quotas prevent most Asians from immigrating to the United States.

1929 The 1924 quotas are made permanent, slowing immigration for 40 years.

1939 Congress does not pass a bill that would have allowed World War II refugees to enter the United States.

1943 The Chinese Exclusion law is repealed.

1948 Congress passes the Displaced Persons Act, which in turn allows hundreds of thousands of refugees, mostly from Eastern Europe, to enter the U.S.

1957 President Dwight D. Eisenhower signs the Refugee Escape Act, which allows refugees from Communist and some Middle Eastern countries to be admitted into the U.S.

1965 President Lyndon B. Johnson and Congress rewrite immigration law, allowing for an immigration boom in the last 30 years of the 1900s.

1970s Hundreds of thousands of refugees from Communist countries in Asia and Eastern Europe enter the United States.

1980 During the "Mariel Boat Lift," approximately 125,000 Cubans arrive in the U.S. on 1,700 boats.

1986 The Immigration Reform and Control Act is passed.

2001 After terrorist attacks in the United States, immigration enforcement and policy is criticized.

2004 President George W. Bush introduces a plan to allow "guest workers" to enter the U.S. from Mexico and Central American countries.

2005 Groups of citizens with guns begin patrolling U.S. borders to stop illegal immigration.

2006 People across the U.S. protest plans to strengthen immigration laws and to build a fence along the U.S.-Mexico border.

GLOSSARY

ally person or country working with another for a common goal

border dividing line between countries, states, or other regions

capitalist political system in which people own land and businesses privately

census count of the number of people living in a particular area

citizen member of a country who has the legal right to live there

civil rights individual rights that all members of a society have

colony land not connected to a nation, yet owned and controlled by it

commerce business, trade

communist political system in which the government owns land and businesses

Congress part of the U.S. government that makes the country's laws

constitution system of laws in a country that state the rights of the people and the powers of the government

contiguous sharing a boundary

democracy form of government in which citizens elect their leaders

deport to send people back to their own country

descendant child, grandchild, and future generations after that

economy total of goods and services produced in a country or region

emancipation to free a person from slavery or control

ethnic to do with a group of people sharing the same culture or place of origin

exclude to keep someone from joining

federal central government

frontier area that has not been fully explored

immigrant person who arrives in a new country after leaving his or her homeland

internment camp place where people are sent against their will for a time

land bridge piece of earth that crosses a body of water

literacy ability to read and write

migration act of moving from one country or region to another

nativist person who dislikes immigrants

natural resource material found in nature that is necessary or useful

nutrient thing in food that is needed by people and animals to stay healthy

political relating to the government

prohibit stop or ban officially

prosperity success, wealth

quota fixed amount of something

racism belief that a particular race is better than others

refugee person who is forced to leave his or her home because of war, persecution, or natural disaster

settler person who moves from one place into a new region

slavery system of buying, selling, and keeping slaves who were forced to work for their owners for no pay

Soviet Union powerful communist country that included Russia and many smaller nations, and which broke up in 1991

stock market place where stocks are bought and sold

Supreme Court highest court of the U.S. government

territory area of land that is under the control of a foreign government

terrorist someone who uses violence and threats to frighten people into obeying

FURTHER READING

BOOKS

Anderson, Kelly C. *Immigration*. San Diego: Lucent, 1993.

Goldish, Meish. *Immigration: How Should It Be Controlled*. New York: Twenty-First Century Books, 1994.

Hoobler, Dorothy and Thomas. *We Are Americans: Voices of the Immigrant Experience*. New York: Scholastic, 2003.

Isbister, John. *The Immigration Debate: Remaking America*. West Hartford, Conn.: Kumarian, 1996.

Rebman, Renee C. *Life on Ellis Island*. San Diego: Lucent, 2000.

Roleff, Tamara L., ed. *Immigration: Opposing Viewpoints*. San Diego: Greenhaven, 1998.

INTERNET

PBS: Destination America
http://www.pbs.org/destinationamerica/

U.S. Citizenship and Immigration Services
http://uscis.gov/graphics/index.htm

Angel Island Immigration Station
http://www.angelisland.org/immigr02.html

Ellis Island
http://www.ellisisland.org/

INDEX